Ancient
Inca

Archaeology Unlocks the Secrets of the Inca's Past

Ancient Inca

Archaeology Unlocks the Secrets of the Inca's Past

By Beth Gruber

Johan Reinhard, Consultant

NATIONAL
GEOGRAPHIC
Washington, DC

Contents

< Inca textile with the woven image of a god

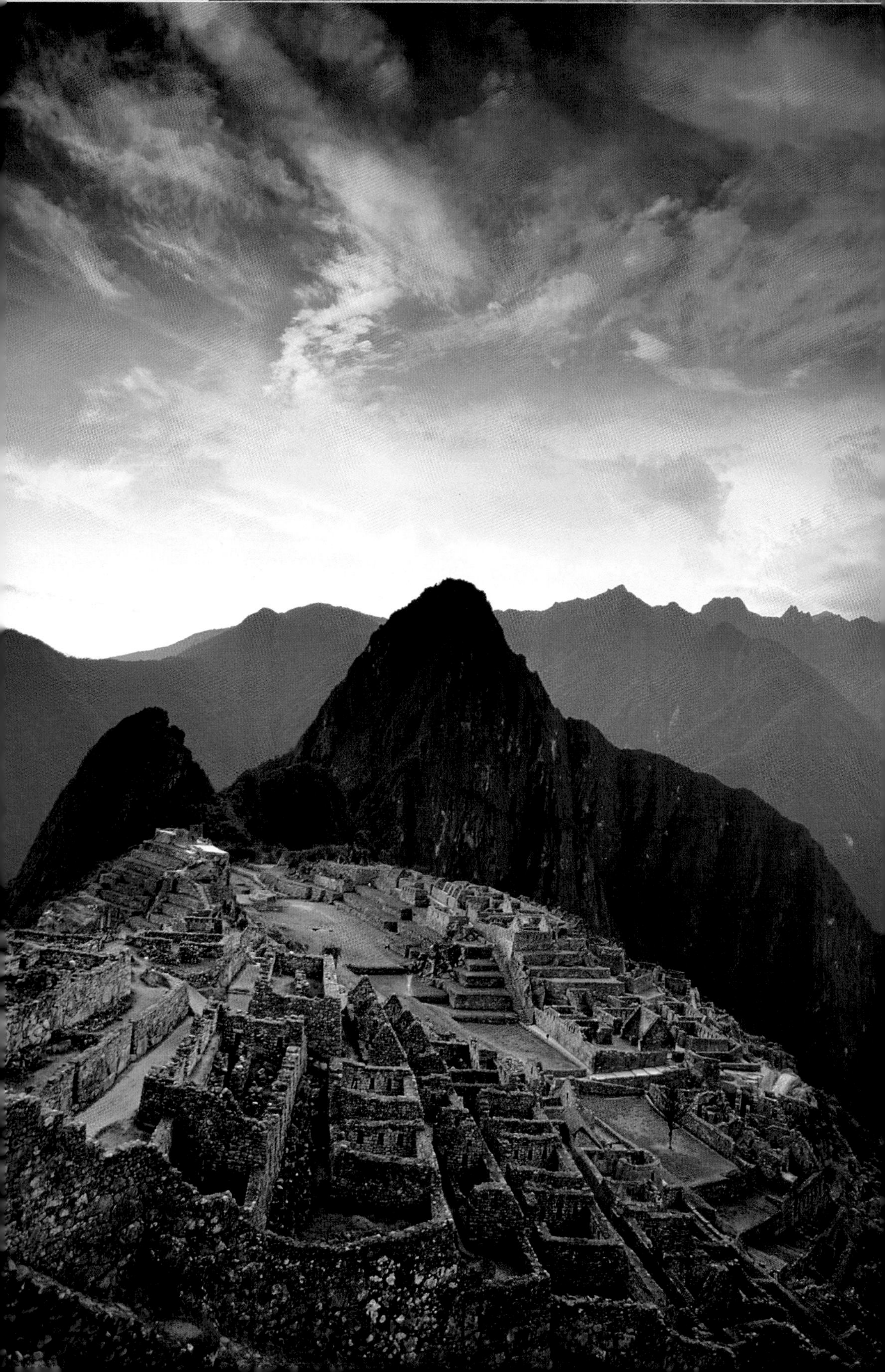

< Ruins at Machu Picchu, a spectacular site where the Inca likely performed spiritual ceremonies

I am honored to have been chosen as a consultant for this book, which brings together some of the latest findings about the Inca. It also points the way to research currently underway that will reveal more secrets about their culture. Before too long, we will even be able to locate their closest living relatives, including those of the frozen Inca mummy nicknamed Juanita. Other mysteries await to be revealed by future archaeologists and scientists from many other fields. Some kinds of research will require explorers to take personal risks, while they investigate isolated and little-known areas of the Andes. Other research will require scientists to use the latest advances in technology to obtain information previously inaccessible to us. For now, I invite you to read this book. Maybe it will prompt you to become one of those who will continue with the exciting process of discovery it describes so well.

Johan Reinhard

< Johan Reinhard examines "Juanita," the Inca mummy he discovered on an Andean mountaintop

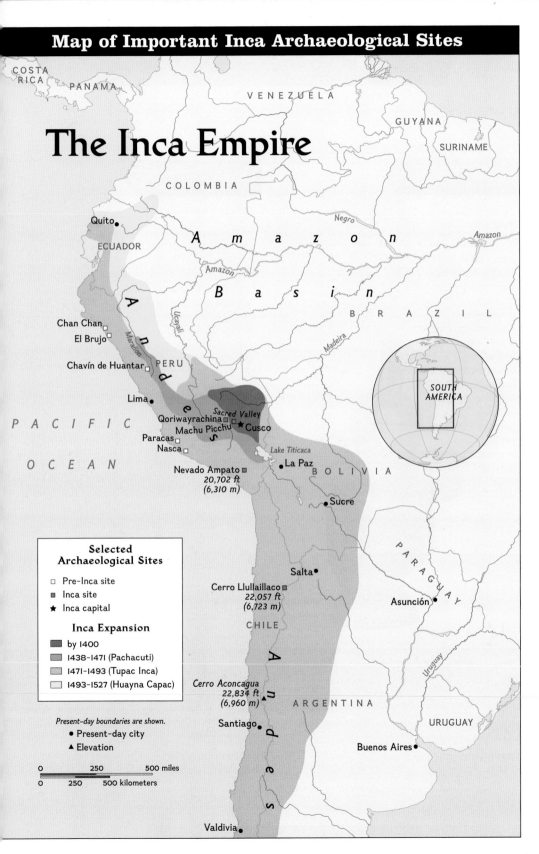

COSTA RICA
PANAMA
VENEZUELA
GUYANA
SURINAME

The Inca Empire

COLOMBIA

Quito
ECUADOR

A m a z o n

Negro

Amazon

Amazon

B a s i n

B R A Z I L

Ucayali

Chan Chan
El Brujo

Marañon

PERU

Chavín de Huantar

Madeira

Lima

Qoriwayrachina
Machu Picchu
Paracas
Nasca

Sacred Valley
★ Cusco

Lake Titicaca

P A C I F I C

Nevado Ampato
20,702 ft
(6,310 m)

La Paz
B O L I V I A

O C E A N

Sucre

SOUTH
AMERICA

P A R A G U A Y

Selected Archaeological Sites

□ Pre-Inca site
▣ Inca site
★ Inca capital

Inca Expansion

- by 1400
- 1438–1471 (Pachacuti)
- 1471–1493 (Tupac Inca)
- 1493–1527 (Huayna Capac)

Present-day boundaries are shown.
- Present-day city
▲ Elevation

Salta

Cerro Llullaillaco
22,057 ft
(6,723 m)

Asunción

CHILE

Uruguay

Cerro Aconcagua
22,834 ft
(6,960 m)

A R G E N T I N A

URUGUAY

A n d e s

Santiago

Buenos Aires

0   250   500 miles
0   250   500 kilometers

Valdivia

Peoples of Peru

SOUTH
AMERICA

Moche

ca 200 B.C. — A.D. 700

In the first century A.D. a culture rose to dominate Peru's northeast coast. It is known as the Moche from its capital, in the valley of the Moche River. The Moche diverted rivers to provide water for crops. They also made realistic pottery vessels. A warlike people, the Moche buried their warriors with great ceremony. They sacrificed prisoners of war and drank their blood.

Chimú

ca A.D. 1100 — 1470

The Chimú may have originated after about 1100. From their capital, Chan Chan, they expanded their power in the 13th century. They built many cities and made massive irrigation works to support their growing population. In the 1460s they were overthrown by the Inca, who adopted the Chimú road system and political organization.

< Moche vessel portraying a warrior in a headdress

Timeline of Peruvian History

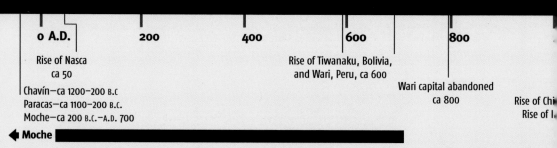

o A.D.   200   400   600   800

Rise of Nasca
ca 50

Rise of Tiwanaku, Bolivia, and Wari, Peru, ca 600

Wari capital abandoned
ca 800

Chavín—ca 1200–200 B.C
Paracas—ca 1100–200 B.C.
Moche—ca 200 B.C.–A.D. 700

Rise of Chi
Rise of I

◀ Moche

Early Inca

ca A.D. 1100—1463

from their capital at Cusco the Inca expanded to dominate the Cusco valley and the Urubamba Valley, which was an important route to Lake Titicaca. They fought many wars with neighboring peoples to cement their control of the region.

Late Inca

A.D. 1463—1532

The emperor Pachacuti and his son, Tupac Inca, waged major wars of conquest, defeating both the Queche and the Chimú. At the height of Inca power in 1525, the empire numbered 8 to 10 million people who spoke at least 20 languages. The Inca had conquered and included in its empire about 100 different peoples.

> Carved knife from the Chimú capital at Chan Chan

< Shell llama from the early Inca period

| 1200 | 1400 | 1600 | 1800 | A.D. 2000 |

Machu Picchu built ca 1450

Collapse of Inca 1532

Pachacuti begins his rule 1438

Tupac Inca extends empire 1471–1493

Peruvian independence 1812

d; pac peror

Virococha becomes emperor ca 1390

Yesterday Comes Alive

CHAPTER 1

How do we learn what we know about the past?

The ancient Inca of Peru had no formal alphabet or system of writing. They did not leave archives for historians to study. The Inca made knots in colored strings called quipus to record the calendar or keep a count of livestock. The first Europeans to meet the Inca were amazed that they could run a huge empire using strings to keep records. Archaeologists have found many ancient quipus—but today no one knows what the knots mean. Without anyone who can read the stories tied into the colorful strings, understanding the ancient Inca is a lot like solving a mystery.

< Archaeologists in Peru sometimes need a head for heights: This Inca burial site is on top of Nevado Ampato, a 20,702-foot (6,310-meter) mountain in the Andes.

So how do we know about a civilization that for nearly a hundred years (1438–1532) ruled a South American empire that rivaled the expanse of ancient Rome? Clues left behind by the Inca form an amazing portrait of their religion, art and architecture, agriculture, government, transportation, and way of life. By studying these clues, archaeologists and others can piece together details of Inca life.

Some of what we know about the Inca comes from oral history, or stories passed from generation to generation. Passing on the stories was an important way to preserve a community's history.

We know some of the old stories because they were written down by the Europeans who arrived in the empire in 1532. The visitors were Spanish soldiers and priests. They described the Inca in letters and diaries.

Historians have to be careful when they interpret these accounts. The Spaniards did not speak the Inca language well. They may not have

The Inca used quipus to keep records. A Spanish visitor made the drawing at right to show the knotted strings being used—the Spaniards could not believe their eyes!

Digging is a careful process where every find has to be precisely recorded.

understood what the Inca told them, so their descriptions might not be accurate. And some of the Inca stories were legends rather than history.

The rest of our knowledge of the Inca comes from artifacts, or objects that they left behind, and from the sites where artifacts are found. As in many ancient civilizations, Inca artifacts might be objects made from stone, pottery, gold, or silver. Such materials last a long time, even if they have been buried for hundreds of years. Some artifacts turn up in the ruins of buildings. Others are found buried in graves for the dead to use in the afterlife.

Some Inca textiles and clothing have also survived remarkably well. Ancient materials like cloth are usually destroyed by dampness, but these have been preserved in the dry deserts on Peru's coasts or the cold mountains of the Andes.

Some Inca sites have been disturbed by treasure hunters or looters, who take anything that might be valuable. Some treasures were taken centuries ago, but looting still goes on today. Looted sites often do not tell archaeologists very much. Other sites are reported to archaeologists, who can dig them up carefully. They provide the best idea of all about life in Peru before and during Inca rule.

Archaeologists who study these sites keep careful records. They write down and photograph any artifacts they find, and note the exact position in which they find them. They need to

∧ Many people in modern Peru are descended from the Inca. They keep the memory of their ancestors alive by re-creating their ceremonies, sue as this sun-worshiping ritual.

learn as much information as they car from every single piece of evidence.

Archaeologists can compare what they learn from artifacts and sites wit the Spaniards' accounts of the Inca. Sometimes archaeology confirms the historical record. In chapter 3, for example, you'll learn about the great Inca capital at Cusco, which amazed the Spaniards with its wealth and grand buildings. Archaeologists have shown that the ancient city was just s spectacular as the awestruck isitors reported.

Among the most important things o learn about a civilization are where came from and what happened to it. he fall of the Inca is easy to date, ecause the Spaniards murdered the ist Inca king in 1532 and took over ne empire. The origins of the Inca are iore difficult to trace. The area where ley lived had long been inhabited by ifferent peoples. Archaeologists have o be careful to make sure exactly hich people built which site. In hapter 2, you will learn about how rchaeologists use some of the most dvanced techniques in the world to iscover more about the Inca's redecessors. You'll see how aerial hotography can help them find atterns in ancient monuments that ley cannot see from the ground.

The Inca lived high in the ndes and may even have orshiped some mountain eaks. Many of their sites re in remote, high places. ome Inca were buried in aves in cliff faces, for xample, or on mountain ips. This has helped to reserve the sites, ecause looters cannot asily get to them. But also makes the job of

Small gold figures were often cluded in the burials of Inca ngs. This statue represents a male god.

∧ Putting together the pieces of this pre-Inca headdress is like doing a jigsaw puzzle—but without a picture on the box to help.

the archaeologist more difficult. In chapter 5 you'll meet high-altitude archaeologists who are expert mountaineers. They have to carry all their equipment up a mountain before they can start work. Anything they find has to be carried down the mountain for study.

The cold mountains act like a giant freezer. Bodies found in the icy Andes are in such good shape that experts can use modern medical scanning equipment to learn about how the people died. The bodies also reveal information about how they lived. Chapter 5 will show you some of the results.

The Inca's Ancestors

CHAPTER 2

How do we know who lived in Peru before the Inca?

Before the Inca emerged in the 12th century, many other peoples had come and gone in the region. In the first half of the 20th century, archaeologists began to untangle the order in which these peoples lived, by studying changes in buildings or in objects such as plates and bowls. It was a tough task: Some sites were used by many different peoples over time.

< Archaeologists remove a layer of cotton from a bundle containing a 1,600-year-old Moche mummy from northern Peru.

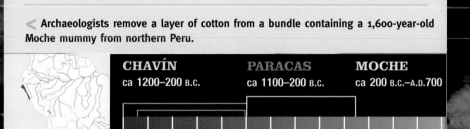

CHAVÍN	PARACAS	MOCHE
ca 1200–200 B.C.	ca 1100–200 B.C.	ca 200 B.C.–A.D.700

| 1200 | 600 | B.C. 0 A.D. | 800 | 1400 |

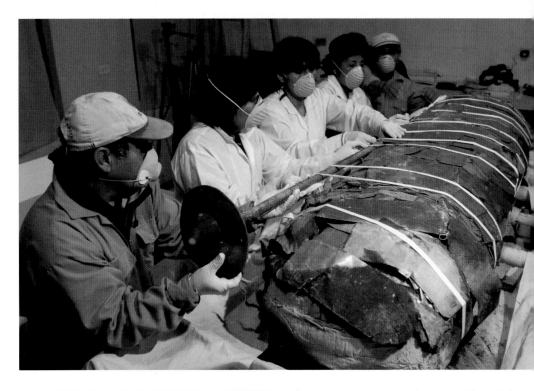

∧ The team removes a giant war club sealed inside the mummy bundle by a layer of sheets made from copper and gold.

Even well-explored sites still have secrets. In 2006, archaeologist Régulo Franco explored a decorated terrace a a site named El Brujo, or the Wizard, overlooking the Pacific Ocean on the north coast of Peru. A thousand years before the Incas rose to power, El Brujo was a site where the warlike Moche people prayed to their gods an performed human sacrifice. Franco discovered that the patio held four tombs, and decided to excavate the largest. His team removed six layers of mud bricks, a scaffolding made of can

< The mummy's tattoos show spiders and snake Experts think the animals might have been linked to harvest ceremonies.

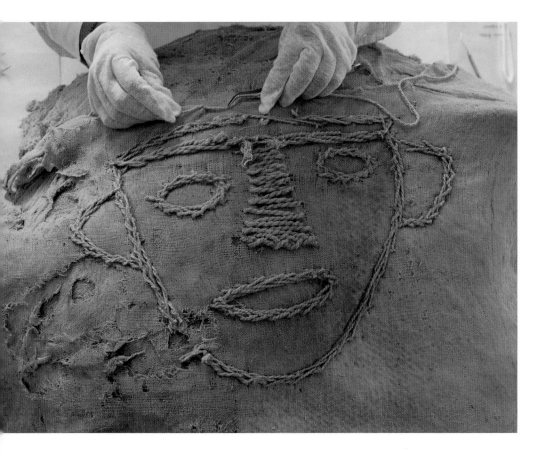

and a reed mat covering six tree
trunks. Beneath the trees lay a large
textile bundle. It was an exciting find:
similar bundles at other sites had
contained the bodies of Moche kings.

The Mummy's Secret

The team moved the bundle to a
laboratory, where textile experts peeled
away the outer layers of cloth. Beneath
was a layer of thin metal sheets made
from gold and copper, and two war
clubs that kings used for ceremonies.
The body itself lay within more layers
of cloth and a layer of gold. It had been
so well preserved by the dry heat of
the coast that the team could still see

A weaving expert works on a thread portrait
embroidered on the outside of the mummy bundle.

the tattoos on its arms. A golden bowl
hid its face, and beads and ornaments
lay near its neck. They included a
small figure of a warrior that
convinced Franco that he had found
the body of an important king.

But when the team took away the
golden bowl from the mummy's face,
two long braids of black hair tumbled
out. Braids were the traditional
hairstyle of Moche women. An
examination revealed that the mummy
was indeed female. She had been
buried so that people could honor her

∧ There are 130 million bricks in the Huaca del Sol. It is slowly crumbling away—but it won't fall down any time soon.

> A Moche portrait cup with a realistic face and a spout for drinking.

shown below. Potters provided a realistic portrait of how the Moche looked and how they lived. Their bottles show men carrying gourds with offerings for the gods, women looking after the sick, even a man chewing coca leaves with lime to take away the bitter taste. Modern inhabitants of the Andes still use coca leaves to combat the effects of living at high altitudes. Another bottle is in the shape of a llama carrying large jars in bags slung across its back. Llamas are still used as pack animals in the Andes, and for their wool and meat. Other pots show warriors smashing their war clubs on their enemies' heads.

The largest physical trace of the Moche is the Huaca del Sol, or Pyramid of the Sun. Built of about 130 million sun-dried adobe bricks, it is one of South America's largest ancient monuments. Its very size is evidence of a powerful culture, organized enough to build something so enormous.

by leaving offerings on the terrace above. Franco believes that the care with which she was buried means that the woman may have been a ruler. This caused archaeologists to think again about the Moche. They had assumed that such a warlike people must have been led by men.

Brick Makers and Potters

The Moche lived in the river valleys of northern Peru from roughly 200 B.C. to A.D. 700. Their graves contain elaborate metalwork and decorative pottery, including "portrait vessels" like the one

A Remarkable Find

New discoveries have led experts back before the Moche, to the first societies in Peru. The ruins of Chavín

e Huántar, in the northern highlands
Peru, hold the remains of two
mples built by the Inca's earliest
ncestors, the Chavín. The site has
een investigated since 1995 by a team
om Stanford University led by
rofessor John Rick. Rick's passion for
arning about the civilizations of the
egion was sparked by a remarkable
nd. When he visited Peru on vacation
age six, Rick and his mother found a
,500-year-old mummy buried in the
nd near the coast north of Lima!

The Old Temple at Chavín de
uántar conceals a buried maze of

passages and chambers that have been
built over by later peoples. Rick and
his team had to work out which parts
were built by the Chavín. They also
had to map the confusing layout of the
site. Regular instruments did not fit
into tight underground spaces, so the
team designed a special version of a
surveying instrument named a
theodolite. It allowed them to take
precise measurements of the small
spaces. They fed the data through a
computer to generate the first accurate
3D map of the temple.

Gods, Rulers, and Farmers

Inside the temple chambers are
carvings of strange humans with
catlike faces. One of the Old Temple's
chambers contains the Lanzon. This
granite figure with clawed feet, snake
hair, and earrings may have been one
of the Chavín's gods. The Gallery of
Offerings was filled with hundreds of
bits of broken pottery decorated with
simple forms. There were also human
remains, evidence of ritual offerings
that may have included people.

Rick discovered that the ruins at
Chavín de Huántar were older than
anyone had thought. From their
appearance, they seemed to date back
to about 1200 B.C., and showed that
the Chavín were an advanced society.
They must have had rulers who could
command laborers to build the

⊲ The 14-foot 6-inch (4.5-meter) high Lanzon
stands in a chamber of the Old Temple. It might
show one of the Chavín's gods.

<Unwrapping a bundled-up mummy from Paracas. The outer layer is made from colorful feathers. The inner layers were made from patterned cloth.

temples, skilled workers like carvers and potters, and priests to carry out their rituals. They must also have had skilled farmers to grow enough food to support everyone. Rick believes that the Chavín may have moved from another part of the continent. Their temples have carvings of alligators and monkeys, which did not live in Peru, but were common in the forests to the east.

It would have taken take hundreds of years for the Chavín to add the New Temple to the complex. The two temples and their plazas formed a center for one of the largest civilizations to inhabit Peru before the Inca came to power.

∧ Detail of clothing from a mummy in Paracas.

Weaving a Story

To the south of Chavín de Huántar is Paracas, a fishing village that was home to another important pre-Inca civilization from roughly 1100 to 200 B.C. Here, archaeologists found tombs that contain hundreds of mummies wrapped in layers of cloth. The mummies were well preserved, thanks to the dry climate. Many of the textiles in which they were wrapped were woven with intricate

Aerial Photography

Archaeologists use aerial photography to study features like the Nasca lines. The images reveal the outlines of sacred animals and other designs that are almost impossible to see from the ground. Some of the lines seem to align with sky features such as stars.

Aerial photographs also show other hidden features. They reveal old earthworks, such as roads or boundaries between fields. The foundations of ancient structures also sometimes show up, such as circular patterns in northern Europe left by ceremonial structures called henges.

⋀ This huge hummingbird drawn on the surface of the Nasca desert can only be seen from the air. Pilots flying aircraft in Peru in the 1920s were the first people in the modern age to draw attention to the Nasca lines.

figures, such as priests or animals. They are the work of a culture whose people were skilled weavers, and who celebrated the connection between humans and the natural world.

Lines in the Sand

Farther south still is Nasca, where puzzling line drawings of birds, fish, monkeys, plants, spiders, and a whale have been etched across more than 800 miles (1300 km) of desert. The stump of a tree felled when the lines were made gave archaeologists the chance to work out their age. They used radiocarbon dating, which measures the decay of carbon 14, a radioactive type of carbon that decays

Fact versus Fiction

Even though myths are sometimes unrealistic, they often contain hidden facts that provide important clues for archaeologists. There probably was an Inca named Manco Capac, for example, and he probably was the leader of his tribe. His name, Capac, became the title for a warlord or king in Quechua, the ancient Inca language that is used to this day.

Language is also a valuable source of information about the past. For example, the Quechua word for a mayor or local ruler is "sinchi." It comes from the name of Manco Capac's son, Sinchi Roca, who is the first figure in Inca myth whose existence can be supported historically. Chronicles created by the Spanish note that Sinchi Roca was the second ruler of the great Inca Empire.

the Spaniards arrived, they wrote down and illustrated these stories. Other stories were passed from generation to generation by descendants of the Inca. Almost all of these records were created after the Inca Empire fell. Most combine fact and legend, and may not be reliable accounts of what really happened.

In one legend about the Inca, a man named Tici Viracocha sends his four sons and four daughters on a quest to establish a village. Along the way, Viracocha's son Manco and daughter Ocllo have a child named Sinchi Roca, who leads them to the valley of Cusco, where the new village is founded. Manco becomes the ruler of the village, and comes to be known as Manco Capac.

at a regular speed. All living things contain carbon, so the technique can date any material that was once alive, such as wood. The tests dated the tree and the lines to around A.D. 500. Were the lines a form of Nasca storytelling, a symbol of religious worship, or an early astronomical calendar? No one knows for sure.

The Origin of the Inca

Other cultures rose and fell in Peru in the following centuries, including the Chimú, who built a vast capital at Chan Chan. Eventually, they would all be eclipsed by the greatest Andean empire of them all: the Inca.

The Inca left many legends about how their empire was created. When

True Story?

What do we know for sure? Excavations in the southern Peruvian highlands indicate that the Inca were a small tribe who made their

> This ceremonial knife depicts a warrior. It belonged to the Chimú, the most powerful of the peoples conquered by the Inca.

< Manco Capac holds an image of the sun in this picture painted by 18th-century Inca descendants.

ome around Cusco some time during
he 13th century. Ruins there are not
ery sophisticated and paint a picture
f a tribe that had humble beginnings.

The power of the Inca grew over
he next two centuries. The accurate
istory of the Inca empire begins with
'achacuti, who ruled from 1438 to
471. Pachacuti's army was strong and
vell armed. Archaeologists have found
olden earrings showing warriors with
pears and shields, and weapons
ncluding woolen slings and clubs with

bronze or stone heads. Remains of
braided cane helmets and armorlike
wooden backplates provide a further
glimpse of what warriors wore in
battle. Seventeenth-century Spanish
drawings complete the picture of
a powerful army that eventually
conquered all of the Inca's neighbors.

The Inca believed that they were
the greatest of all civilizations, and
that other peoples were savages. In a
short time they conquered an area that
included what are now Peru, Bolivia,
and Ecuador, and parts of Chile and
Argentina. At their height, they ruled
between eight and 10 million people in
an empire that was almost as vast as
the distance from the east to west
coasts in the United States!

∨ Messengers from other peoples bring gifts to
the Inca emperor, who carries a ceremonial war club
with a golden tip. At right, an official ties knots in
quipus to record the gifts.

All Roads Go to Cusco

CHAPTER 3

How did engineering help the Inca rule their empire?

It seems only natural that all roads would lead to Cusco, because it was the heart of the Inca Empire. And what roads they were! Stretching some 10,000 to 14,000 miles (16,000 to 22,500 km), the Inca road system was a marvel of engineering. It crossed great distances and spanned many obstacles. It reached high into the mountains, into the jungles, and across the desert.

< Inca roads were once used only by imperial messengers. Now farmers drive their animals along them.

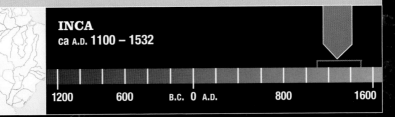

INCA
ca A.D. 1100 – 1532

| 1200 | 600 | B.C. 0 A.D. | 800 | 1600 |

The Inca walls of Cusco are so well built that it's impossible even to slide a piece of paper between the huge, oddly shaped stones.

Military roads were wide enough for armies to march along. In the desert, roads were built with walls to keep sand off them. Most roads had regular rest houses or way stations called *tambos*, where official messengers and important travelers could rest overnight.

The navel of the empire

Travelers to Cusco today can still see remains of Inca roads leading into and through the city. People still walk on the same stones where Inca armies and llama trains once traveled!

Cusco means "navel" in the Quechua language. The city high in the Andes was the center of the empire that the Inca called Tahuantinsuyu, o Land of the Four Quarters. Home to the Inca king and the royal family, it was also the seat of a government tha oversaw all of the Inca Empire.

Later inhabitants have built on top of the ancient buildings in Cusco, but visitors can still see Inca walls at the base of newer buildings. The huge stones in the walls fit together so snugly that it is impossible to slide even a thin piece of paper between them. Even though they are held together without mortar, the walls are strong enough to have withstood 500 years of earthquakes!

The Temple of the Sun

n central Cusco lie the remains of he Inca's most spectacular place of worship, the Coricancha, or Temple of the Sun. But one must look closely. Gone are the gardens' life-size golden culptures of animals and corn the Spanish chroniclers wrote about with awe. The Spaniards took most of the golden objects to melt down. Gone oo is the huge monument to the sun,

> Church in Cusco built on top of the Coricancha.

∨ The Inca capital may have had up to 200,000 residents when the Spaniards arrived. It was 10 imes bigger than the Spanish capital, Madrid.

encrusted with emeralds and other precious stones. Also gone are the observatory and the calendar that the Spaniards learned the Inca used to calculate the changing of the seasons.

All that remains of the original temple are the walls of chambers dedicated to the moon, thunder, and the rainbow. They lie at the center of a church, built on top of the Inca foundations. If it weren't for an earthquake that exposed the walls in 1950, the Coricancha might never have been discovered!

The Great Fortress

Great warriors need a mighty fortress, and no fortress has ever rivaled Sacsahuaman. It is the Inca's greatest building achievement—and one of the most remarkable pieces of architecture ever built. The ruins of the fortress form the centerpiece of a huge archaeological park in Cusco that is filled with clues about the Inca's way of life.

The most impressive section of Sacsahuaman today is the three jagged rows of massive stone walls that rise up on the side of the steep hill overlooking Cusco. They are built with gigantic limestone boulders, some of which weigh up to 70 tons (64 tonnes). Each stone is a different shape, but they all fit precisely together.

Once the citadel was a complex

military center. It had towers, a reservoir to supply water, a palace, storage places for food and weapons, and housing for soldiers. Today all that remains are ruins.

Earth and Water

Other sites in the Sacsahuaman Archaeological Park provide further evidence about how the Inca lived. At Q'Enqo, a semi-circular main building with window seats and an enormous rock that resembles a puma hint at a ceremonial place that might have been used to worship either animals or Mother Earth. Visitors can still see simple drawings of pumas on the walls of the site's twisting underground passages.

A second sanctuary, Tambomachay, has flowing water that falls through a series of channels into a pool at the bottom. Some archaeologists believe the site may have been used by the Inca to perform water rituals.

Who built the fortress?

The Spanish conquistadors were so stunned by the sheer size of Sacsahuaman that they believed it could only have been built by demons. One man, a chronicler named Garcilaso de la Vega, grew up in the shadow of its walls, but could never find a single worker who claimed to have worked at the site.

Historians and scientists have their own theory. They believe it took more than 20,000 men, working for over 60 years, to complete the great fortress. They suggest that workers must have used simple rollers, levers, and scaffolding to move the giant boulders, hand-sized stones to sculpt the rocks into shape, and tracings to copy each boulder's edge so that it would fit neatly with the boulder next to it.

◁ The walls of Sacsahuaman are built in three rows of zig-zags and look like the fearsome teeth of the sacred puma.

▷ Massive stones formed the walls of the fortress at Sacsahuaman.

The Sacred Valley

CHAPTER 4

Why was one small valley home to so many of the Inca's sacred sites?

What makes the Sacred Valley so special? The Sacred Valley is a particularly important location for uncovering the history of the Inca people. Here, along the Urubamba River just 10 miles (16 km) north of Cusco, villagers live amid the legacy of their Inca ancestors, including Machu Picchu, one of the world's greatest archaeological sites.

< Full of golden corn and surrounded by high mountains, the Urubamba Valley was sacred to the Incas.

INCA
ca A.D. 1100 – 1532

| 1200 | 600 | B.C. 0 A.D. | 800 | 1600 |

At the entrance to the Sacred Valley, perched on a mountain ledge high above the market town of Pisac, lies a complex of ruins made of small, polished rocks. The main ruins include temples built to the sun, moon, rainbow, rain, and stars. One temple has a "hitching post." This stone pillar beneath the open sky was probably used to track the movements of important stars to help the Inca calculate the changing seasons.

Steps to the Skies

On the mountainsides around Pisac, the Inca left remains that are just as impressive as the ruined temples— and just as important for Inca life. Huge agricultural terraces a few yards

∧ Terraces on the hillsides high above Pisac are still in use.

> Corn was the Inca's main food. Corn cobs made of silver, like this one, were planted at the temple at Cusco.

ride cover the slopes like a series of steps. Turning the hillside into flat steps allowed the Inca to grow as many crops as possible to feed the hungry population. Corn, which grew in many varieties and colors, was the most important food. Near Pisac, the Inca dug a canal to bring water from the Urubamba River to more fields. They also diverted a salty stream into ponds where the water evaporated, leaving behind piles of salt. For people who ate mainly vegetables and grains, eating extra salt added taste and helped keep bodies healthy. The salt pans are still in use some 500 years after they were first created.

The Inca Retreat

Ollantaytambo, also in the Sacred Valley, is one of the best surviving examples of Inca town planning. Today's town follows the same shape laid out by the Inca. Built on top of Inca foundations and terraces, it is divided into *canchas*, or blocks, which are almost entirely intact. A huge stone doorway marks the entrance to each block, which leads to a central courtyard surrounded by houses.

In the uppermost part of the city lie the remains of a partially built temple. In front of the temple stand six huge, perfect red stones. They

Some unusual Inca terraces are a puzzle. No one knows exactly why they were built in such nearly perfect circles.

> Sure-footed llamas find it easy to climb to Machu Picchu, but few people visited the mountaintop site for centuries.

came from a quarry on the other side of the Urubamba River. Experts think that workers used ramps and rollers to move the stones to where they stand today. They even may have diverted the river so that they would not have to ferry the rocks over it.

Chronicles left by the Spaniards tell us that the last Inca leader, Manco Inca, retreated to Ollantaytambo after Spanish troops defeated him at Sacsahuaman. From great heights, his army showered arrows, spears, and rocks down on the Spanish soldiers. But they could not hold off the Spanish forever. After four attempts, the conquistadors took the town. The remaining Inca moved farther into the mountains. And the great temple was never completed.

The Not-So-Lost City

The most important site in the Sacred Valley was Machu Picchu. Its spectacular mountaintop site high above a bend in the Urubamba has made it one of the most popular tourist attractions in the world. Machu Picchu is often called the "the city in the clouds" or "the lost city of the Inca." But was Machu Picchu ever really lost? Ancient maps marked the site, and local people knew about the ruins. Two brothers lived there as farmers, raising crops and using the old walls as pens for animals. But

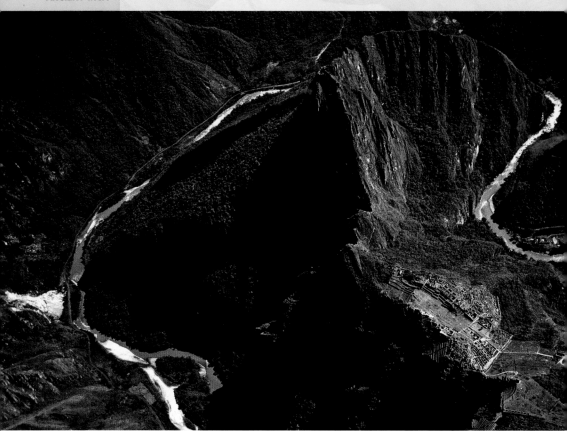

outside the region people had forgotten about the city until it was discovered—or rediscovered—by Hiram Bingham in 1911.

The American archaeologist guessed that Machu Picchu had been partly built by Manco Inca, after he had fled from the Spaniards at Ollantaytambo. No one agrees with Bingham's theory now, but his work helped draw attention to the ancient site. He cleared the vegetation that had overgrown the ruins, and photographed and mapped the site.

A Stunning Site

Machu Picchu is one of the world's most significant archaeological sites. Since Bingham's time, archaeologists

The Urubamba River snakes beneath the mountaintop site of Machu Picchu. Local brothers ran a farm on the remote site before Hiram Bingham's visit in 1911.

have studied there to learn more about the Inca. They are amazed by its design and its remarkable stonework. By talking with modern descendants of the Inca, they hope to discover clues to what life might have been like 500 years ago.

Even after nearly one hundred years' work, there is still much to discover about Machu Picchu. Archaeologists still do not know for sure what it was used for, or who lived there. Some experts think that it might have been used only for ceremonies or by the Inca's rulers.

Spiritual Center

Whatever the city was used for, it had spiritual meaning for the Inca. Visitors to Machu Picchu at sunrise can experience the sun coming up over the surrounding peaks, just as the Inca did centuries ago. Sunrise at Machu Picchu is so breathtaking that it is easy to see why the Inca worshiped the sun and the mountains as powerful gods.

Everything at Machu Picchu appears to have been planned to refer to the mountains or the sky. Its enormous main gate and the entrance corridor that leads to the Sacred Plaza focus on spectacular mountain views. Within the Sacred Plaza, the Temple of the Three Windows looks out over more mountains, and faces the summer solstice. This is the point during the year at which the sun is closest to the Equator. At the far side of the Plaza, the Intimachay, or Cave of the Sun, looks out to the winter solstice, when the sun is farthest from the Equator.

Archaeologists speculate that even the ruined walls, stone monuments, and mysterious caves scattered throughout Machu Picchu all have spiritual or ceremonial significance.

Masters of Stonework

Machu Picchu also has many features common to other Inca towns. Its magnificent agricultural terraces were probably used to grow food for whoever lived in the city. The crops may have included corn, which was used to brew *chicha,* a drink that was offered to the gods.

The stone walls found throughout Machu Picchu are typical of work done by Inca stonemasons. Unlike most stone blocks, however, which have eight corners and six sides, the stone blocks used to build Machu Picchu are polygonal, or many sided. One stone at Machu Picchu is estimated to have 32 corners. Stones shaped like these cannot be seen anywhere else in the world.

Sometime in the 16th century, Machu Picchu was abandoned. We may

Storehouses on the hillside preserved the crops grown on the surrounding terraces to feed the population of Machu Picchu.

Computer Imagery

Computer technology has been a great help for archaeologists. Computers can process data to create maps or analyze the materials in artifacts. They can also help archaeologists show people what they have discovered, which is important for educational purposes—and also helps raise funds for further research. For example, Yale University's Peabody Museum of Natural History in New Haven, Connecticut, staged in 2005 and 2006 an exhibition called *Machu Picchu: Unveiling the Mystery of the Incas*. The exhibition featured a virtual tour of Machu Picchu and the adjacent Inca Trail, which was created by Cal State Hayward (CSUH) archaeology professor George Miller working with a team of CSUH Media Center staff and CSUH graduate students.

Miller's team began by traveling to Peru to take 360-degree digital photographs of the city's agricultural terraces, granite walls, steps, and caves. To get a three-dimensional effect, they used two Olympus digital cameras with wide-angle lenses and special virtual reality equipment. The equipment provided views of the Machu Picchu ruins that the viewer could move around.

After several trips, the team returned to the CSUH New Media Services laboratory, where they electronically "stitched together" more than 5,000 separate images. Then they added a soundtrack that included such sounds as the flow of water through 16 ceremonial fountains, the roar of the Urubamba River, the Quechua language, and footsteps on the 3,000 steps that line the site.

The result was an incredible virtual tour for museum visitors, who could visit points of interest, look skyward, at the ground, or all around—all at the click of a computer mouse!

never know why. It would be hundreds of years before anyone but local people saw Machu Picchu again.

Another Look at the Past

In 1999, British explorer Peter Frost and a colleague were hiking on a ridge about 40 miles (65 km) from Machu Picchu when some ruins caught their eye. The site, Qoriwayrachina, had never been carefully explored. It took Frost two years to organize an expedition sponsored by the National Geographic Society to the remote Vilacamba Mountains. There he and his colleagues found evidence of a settlement with more than 100 structures, including homes, cemeteries, roads, and terraces. An aqueduct had once carried water five miles (eight km) to the site from a lake high up the mountain. The effort taken to build the channel suggested that the site had a special importance.

Old pieces of pottery indicated that the site might have existed before the Inca grew powerful and took it over. The site had a number of attractions for the Inca. There were ancient mine shafts where they dug for minerals such as gold and silver. Some were in use only forty years

The National Geographic team build their camp
or the expedition to Qoriwayrachina.

Pottery drinking cup
discovered at Qoriwayrachina.

go, but the stone
roadway that links them all
together was built by the Inca.
There were corrals where
farmers kept llamas and alpacas
for their meat and wool. In the
valleys, people still grow potatoes and
corn. And there are platforms from
where Frost believes the Inca
worshiped the great peaks
surrounding the site.

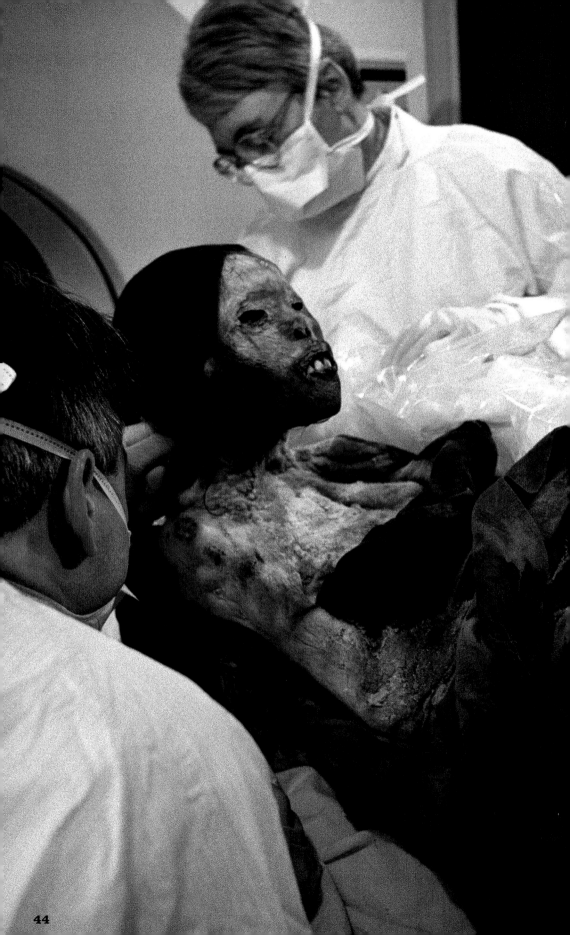

Frozen in Time

What can archaeologists learn from frozen mummies?

The precise location of ceremonial ruins like Machu Picchu are good evidence that mountains were important to the Inca. Perhaps it was because the Andes mountain range was the backbone of their great empire and dominated nearly all of their lands. Or maybe it's because the Inca believed that mountains were not just ladders to their gods, but actually were gods.

< A 500-year-old patient: Medical staff at a U.S. hospital prepare the Inca mummy known as Juanita to enter a CAT scanner.

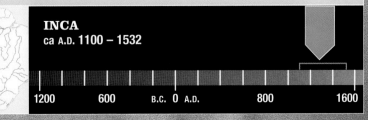

INCA
ca A.D. 1100 – 1532

| 1200 | 600 | B.C. 0 A.D. | 800 | 1600 |

Johan Reinhard approaches an icefield on Nevado Ampato as smoke billows from the volcano Nevado Sabancaya in the distance.

For archaeologists studying the Inca, Andean mountain summits can be a treasure trove. Some Inca sites are easy to get to, and people have looted old graves and ruins looking for valuable objects. The very heights of the mountains make others difficult for treasure hunters to reach, so these sites have a good chance of remaining intact. But they are just as hard to reach for archaeologists. Climbing a mountain requires the strength and conditioning of an athlete. Descending a mountain is dangerous and can even be deadly. A single fall can mean the difference between life and death.

High-altitude archaeologists are specialists who are trained to carry out excavations at extreme heights. One of the world's best-known high-altitude archaeologists, Dr. Johan Reinhard, has led more than 100 expeditions to the peaks of the Andes mountains.

Johan and Juanita

One of Reinhard's most spectacular finds happened unexpectedly in 1995. He and a companion were climbing Nevado Ampato, a volcano in Peru, to get a view of the eruption of a nearby volcano. Reinhard wrapped two stones in yellow plastic to serve as markers and tossed them down into the crater below. Not far from where one of the marker stones landed was a bundle, wrapped in striped cloth and

▼ On later expeditions, Johan Reinhard found three more bodies on Nevado Ampato. One, a girl, was about eight years old. She wore a headdress of feathers that had been squashed down to fit into her grave. The grave itself was lined with red soil carried up from farther down the mountain— red was a sacred color for the Inca. The tomb also contained about 40 artifacts, such as pieces of pottery, spoons, and tools for weaving textiles.

< For her ritual execution, Juanita was dressed in brightly colored clothes held together with silver pins and an elaborate feathered headdress.

perched on a column of ice. Beyond it pieces of torn cloth, a seashell, two cloth bags, llama bones, and Inca pottery lay scattered across the ice.

Reinhard and his companion made the descent down the icy slope, and used an ice pick to free the bundle. When they turned it over, both men were stunned. They were looking at the face of a young girl!

Lessons of Juanita

Juanita, as the girl came to be nicknamed, was the first frozen female mummy ever found in South America. Because her body was frozen, it was like a time capsule. Medical examinations later showed that Juanita had eaten a meal of vegetables about six hours before she died. Her death was caused by a sharp blow on the side of her head. She was wearing clothes made from high-quality textiles. For the first time, experts could see how the Inca wore their *lliclla*, or shawls—folded, wrapped around their shoulders, and fastened with a silver pin.

Children of Llullaillaco

Finding Juanita was only a start. Reinhard found two more children's bodies on Ampato. Four years later, on an expedition with Dr. Constanza Ceruti, he made another startling

Dating Juanita

In May 1996, less than a year after she was discovered on the mountainside, the mummy called Juanita made the long journey from Peru to Johns Hopkins University Hospital in Baltimore, Maryland, where some of the world's most advanced technology awaited.

In the Department of Radiology, CAT scans and computer programs, like the ones used to film the movie *Jurassic Park*, allowed doctors and archaeologists—all wearing special glasses adapted for 3D viewing—to peel away Juanita's clothing and examine her skull, soft tissue, and organs without ever touching her. A fracture near her right eye revealed the cause of Juanita's death, while a piece of tissue taken from her stomach showed traces of vegetables she probably ate within hours of her death.

DNA profiling, performed by experts from the Institute for

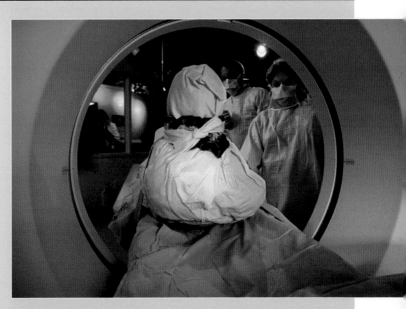

∧ The CAT scanner is normally used to check for signs of disease.

Genomic Research in Rockville, Maryland, disclosed a strain of DNA that has not been reported before. With the profile, scientists hoped they might trace Juanita's relatives who are living today.

By testing the carbon-14 in her hair, doctors determined that Juanita had lived around A.D. 1470, only twenty years before Columbus landed in the Americas. Dental studies place her age around 14 years old. Had she lived in modern times, Juanita probably would have been in high school.

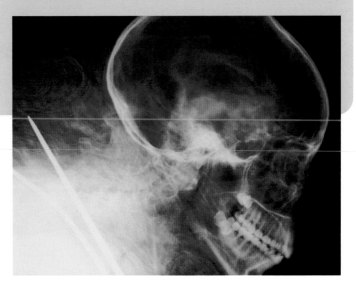

▸ This x-ray shows Juanita's skull and the metal pins that hold together her clothing.

< Archaeologists carefully open a bundle to reveal the face of the youngest of the Llullaillaco children for the first time in 500 years.

∨ The team had to carry everything they found down the mountain on their backs— including the bodies of the three children.

discovery. They climbed Llullaillaco in Argentina to set up the highest archaeological dig in the world. For two days snow kept everyone in their tents before the weather broke and they could climb to the summit. Over the next few days, they discovered not just one frozen mummy, but three!

The children (two girls and a boy) were so well preserved, it was possible to see their expressions and the hair on their arms. Unlike Juanita, they did not seem to have died violently. It is possible that they might have been given alcoholic drinks to make them unconscious. The younger girl had tucked her hands and feet into her clothes, as if to protect herself from the cold. The boy had a pair of sandals and a sling, to take with him to the afterlife.

Presents for the Gods

According to the Spanish, the Inca sacrificed children as special offerings to the gods. It was seen as an honor to make such a sacrifice. Families sometimes even offered their own children, who were led in processions to the mountaintops.

Reinhard found more evidence of this in a small building near the summit, where the priests who carried out the sacrifice must have taken shelter. There was llama dung near the summit, which suggested that the Inca used the animals to carry up building materials and supplies, such as coca used in the rituals.

The small statues buried near the bodies were identical to those found in other parts of the Andes. They were dressed in brightly-colored cloth. Textiles expert William Conklin deduced that they were all likely made in Cusco and distributed throughout the empire. High on a remote mountain, Reinhard had found striking reminders of the Inca empire's reach and power.

< The boy's sandals were of a style common among the Inca.

V The costumes on statues found in the graves are identical to cloth made in Cusco. The textiles were likely woven in the capital.

Meet an Archaeologist

Dr. Constanza Ceruti is a professor at the Catholic University in Salta, Argentina. She is the world's only female high-altitude archaeologist, and was a co-leader on the expedition to Llullaillaco.

◻ What led you to the site at Llullaillaco?

▣ Dr. Reinhard had been exploring the mountain for many years, and I was also looking forward to working on its summit. We believed that, since it is the highest mountain in the area, and the only one with permanent snow on its slopes, it might have been considered very sacred by the Incas. Historical sources written by the Spanish conquerors tell us that the Incas would build shrines and perform offerings on the summits of high snow-capped peaks in the Andes.

◻ What special difficulties are there working at such a site?

▣ We conducted our archaeological work on the Llullaillaco under extreme environmental conditions. There was little oxygen in the air, freezing temperatures, strong winds, and stormy weather. We camped on the ice and had to melt snow in order to get water to drink or to use for cooking. Our food supplies had to be carried up the mountain to higher camps. Consequently we ended up climbing the mountain several times before we actually started scientific work on the summit.

◻ How did you get the mummies down the mountain?

▣ The mummies and other artifacts had to be carried down the dangerous slopes of the volcano on our shoulders. We wrapped them in insulating material to protect them from the sun. At the foot of the mountain, they were put in containers filled with dry ice and driven in military vehicles to the city of Salta.

◻ What happened to them then?

▣ For the next five years, we studied the mummies and other artifacts at the Catholic University of Salta. Radiologists, dentists, pathologists, and other archaeologists helped with ur work. Teamwork is very nportant to archaeological vork. I am very grateful to hese professionals and to he Peruvian students and nountain guides in Dr. einhard's team who made a ital contribution to the uccess of the Llullaillaco xpedition.

] What special skills does high-altitude archaeologist eed?
] A high-altitude rchaeologist needs to be a rofessional archaeologist nd an experienced mountain limber. When we explore eaks like the Andes in South America, we usually work at n elevation above 16,500 eet (5,000 meters), where here is danger of being ffected by mountain ickness.

] When did you first vant to be a high-altitude rchaeologist?
] In spite of the dangers of ur work, I have wanted to be high-altitude archaeologist ince I was a child.

] How do you get ready for our expeditions?
] I prepare for high-altitude xpeditions by regularly limbing smaller peaks and valking long distances to get in shape. I also read nany historical sources and ublications about the area am exploring.

⋀ **An expedition tent beneath the summit of Llullaillaco**

Some mountains are so remotely located that we usually have little information on what we are likely to find.

◙ What happens to the things you find?
▣ My work is funded by a grant from the National Council of Scientific Research in Argentina. I present my projects and get permits for the archaeological excavations I undertake. Periodically, I hand in reports on the results of my excavations, so that the archaeological sites we discover can be protected against treasure hunting and looting. The items we recover are handed over to authorities

to be preserved. Sometimes local authorities will decide to display the findings in a local museum.

◙ Do you spend all your time up a mountain?
▣ When I am not working with an archaeological expedition, I write books and scientific publications about the mountaintop sites that I have explored in Argentina. When I am not in the mountains, I may be anywhere in the world, attending a symposium on Andean archaeology—or a congress on mummies!

Rescuing the Past

CHAPTER 6

Is there still more to learn about the Inca?

Exploring the ancient Inca is a little bit like reading a story. Each new chapter, or discovery, reveals something new or helps us to better understand something we were not sure of before. Archaeologists are the authors of this story. But time is not on their side.

The end of the Inca Empire came quickly. Near the end of the 1400s, Spanish explorers arrived in South America. They brought terrible diseases, including smallpox and measles, that killed millions of people. They also sent reports back to Spain of golden riches beyond imagination.

< Archaeologist Peter Lerche hangs by a rope to check that a cliff-face tomb in the Chachapoya region has not been looted. Grave robbing is a serious problem in Peru.

In 1532, Francisco Pizarro and other Spanish conquistadors came in search of this gold. They trapped the emperor, Atahuallpa. He collected huge amounts of gold and silver from all over the empire, and offered it in return for his life. Pizarro took the gold, but killed Atahuallpa anyway.

∧ **The Spanish used llamas to steal the Inca's treasures.**

The conquistadors drove the next emperor, Manco Inca, into the mountains. They looted everything they could find and sent the riches back to Spain. They used the great stones from Inca buildings to build their own homes. Before long, the records written by the Spaniards were almost all that was left of the once-great Inca Empire.

Tomb robbers

Today, treasure hunters, tourism, development, and the elements pose

as much of a threat to remaining Inca ruins as Pizarro and his soldiers once did. Grave robbers, or *huaqueros*, make a living by selling precious artifacts they take from ceremonial graveyards. But they are not the only ones. Grave robbing is now a national pastime that is tied to the religious calendar. It is at its worst around Easter. During Holy Week, families hold picnics atop ancient Inca cemeteries. Young and old alike dig the ground, searching for trinkets and treasures even though they are breaking the law.

Tourism is another threat to Inca ruins. On the Inca Trail that leads to Machu Picchu there is already a daily limit on the number of visitors. Some scientists worry that visitors to Machu Picchu might cause erosion that would lead to landslides.

Local development at busy places like Cusco and Pisac have created new cities on top of sites that were once great Inca cities. And erosion and the elements threaten pre-Inca sites, such as Chavín de Huántar and Chan Chan.

Saving Inca Heritage

Organizations like the United Nations Educational, Scientific and Cultural Organization (UNESCO) are

acing against time to recognize
endangered sites of cultural or
natural importance around the
world. They fund efforts to preserve
them. Inca ruins classed by UNESCO
as World Heritage sites include
Chan Chan, Chavín de Huántar,
Cusco, and Machu Picchu.

There are other positive signs. In
South American countries, museums
are using exciting ways to show people
Inca treasures. They have to find ways
to put fragile items on display that do
not hinder attempts to preserve them.
In Salta, Argentina, the remarkable
Museo de Arqueología de Alta
Montaña preserves the Llullaillaco
findings. Hopefully, visitors will one
day be able to get close enough to the
three Llullaillaco mummies to see
where lightning struck the eldest girl,
burning her skin and clothing. Her
bright feathered headdress looks as if
it had been made only yesterday.

∧ ∨ **Two problems that threaten records of Peru's past: a looted grave (*above*) and overcrowding at Machu Picchu (*below*).**

As civilizations go, the Inca
Empire did not last very long. But
the dedicated work of archaeologists
means that the mark it left on history
will not soon be forgotten.

The Years Ahead

⋀ Peruvians celebrate their Inca heritage in Cusco with a parade through the streets in a re-creation of Inti Raymi, an ancient festival dedicated to the sun.

Archaeologists in Peru are putting ancient objects back in the hands of local people. Museums display them in cities like Cusco. That helps Peruvians understand their rich heritage while preserving it at the same time. Local people are also training to become experts, to help more Peruvians find out about their Inca ancestors.

Glossary

adobe – a brick made of dried earth and straw

afterlife – an existence after death

architect – a person who designs buildings or gives advice on their construction

artifact – any object changed by human activity

astronomical – relating to the study of objects outside the Earth's atmosphere

carbon-14 – a form of the element carbon, found in all living things; it can be used to date objects accurately

CAT scan – a 3 D image made by x-ray cameras and computers

ceramics – objects made from clay

chicha – a brew made from corn, used as an offering to the gods

chronicle – a record of historical events, written as they occurred

circa – about; used to indicate a date that is approximate and abbreviated as ca

citadel – a stronghold or fortress

conquistador – a leader or soldier in the Spanish conquest of South America

corral – an enclosure, usually for keeping animals

excavation – an archaeological dig

looters – robbers; people who steal objects of value

mortar – a building material, like cement, that hardens to hold objects together

oral history – stories that are passed from generation to generation by word of mouth

pathologist – a scientist who studies the nature of disease

polygonal – many-sided

puma – a large wildcat, also known as a cougar

Quechua – the language of the ancient Incas

quipu – a colorful knotted string used by ancient Inca to keep records

reservoir – a place for storing a liquid such as water

rituals – repeated practices that relate to specific ceremonies

summit – the highest point

terraces – a series of horizontal platforms built on a hillside

textiles – woven or knit cloth

theory – an explanation that fits all of the known evidence

Bibliography

Books

Baquedano, Elizabeth. *Aztec, Inca & Maya*. New York: Dorling Kindersley, 1993.

Mann, Elizabeth. *Machu Picchu*. New York: Mikaya Press, 2000.

Reinhard, Johan. *Discovering the Inca Ice Maiden: My Adventures on Ampato*. Washington, D.C.: National Geographic Society, 1998.

Shuter, Jane. *The Incas*. Chicago: Heinemann Library, 2002.

Wood, Tim. *The Incas*. New York: Viking, 1996.

Articles

Donnan, Christopher B. "Masterworks of Art Reveal a Remarkable Pre-Inca World." NATIONAL GEOGRAPHIC (June 1990): 16–29.

Frost, Peter. "Mystery Mountain of the Inca." NATIONAL GEOGRAPHIC (February 2004): 66–81.

Reinhard, Johan. "Frozen in Time." NATIONAL GEOGRAPHIC (November 1999): 36–55.

Reinhard, Johan. "New Inca Mummies." NATIONAL GEOGRAPHIC (July 1998): 128–135

Williams, A.R. "Mystery of the Tattooed Mummy." NATIONAL GEOGRAPHIC (June 2006): 70–83.

Further Reading

Calvert, Patricia. *The Ancient Inca* (People of the Ancient World). New York: Franklin Watts, 2004.

Sanders, Nicholas J. *The Inca City of Cuzco* (Places in History). Milwaukee Wis.: World Almanac Library, 2005.

Somervill, Barbara. *Machu Picchu: City in the Clouds* (Digging Up the Past). New York: Children's Press, 2005.

On the Web

Ice Mummies of the Inca
http://www.pbs.org/wgbh/nova/icemummies

Ice Treasures of the Inca
http://www.nationalgeographic.com/mummy

MAAM SALTA: Museo de Arqueología de Alta Montaña
http://www.maam.org.ar/

UNESCO World Heritage List for Peru
http://whc.unesco.org/en/statesparties/pe

ndex

About the Author

BETH GRUBER is a graduate of the New York University School of Journalism. She has worked in children's publishing for more than 20 years as an author, editor, and reviewer of books for young readers. She has written a second book for National Geographic titled *Countries of the World: Mexico*.

Consultant

JOHAN REINHARD is an explorer-in-residence at the National Geographic Society and is also a senior research fellow at The Mountain Institute, West Virginia. He is a visiting professor at the Catholic University, Salta, Argentina, and an honorary professor at the Catholic University, Arequipa, Peru. He has led more than 100 high-altitude archaeological expeditions in the Andes and the Himalaya. In 2000 *Outside Magazine* selected him as one of the world's "25 most extraordinary adventurers, outdoor athletes, and explorers."

◁ Inca pottery vase showing the face of a noble

One of the world's largest nonprofit
scientific and educational organizations, the
National Geographic Society was founded in
1888 "for the increase and diffusion of
geographic knowledge." Fulfilling this
mission, the Society educates and inspires millions
every day through its magazines, books, television
programs, videos, maps and atlases, research grants,
the National Geographic Bee, teacher workshops, and
innovative classroom materials. The Society is
supported through membership dues, charitable gifts,
and income from the sale of its educational products.
This support is vital to National Geographic's mission
to increase global understanding and promote
conservation of our planet through exploration,
research, and education.

For more information, please call 1-800-NGS-LINE
(647-5463) or write to the following address:

National Geographic Society
1145 17th Street N.W.
Washington, D.C. 20036-4688
U.S.A.

Visit the Society's Web site:
www.nationalgeographic.com

Library of Congress Cataloging-in-Publication Data
available upon request
Hardcover ISBN-10: 0-7922-7827-5
         ISBN-13: 978-0-7922-7827-6
Library Edition ISBN-10: 0-7922-7873-9
         ISBN-13: 978-0-7922-7873-3

Printed in Mexico

Series design by Jim Hiscott
The body text is set in Century Schoolbook
The display text is set in Helvetica Neue, Clarendon

National Geographic Society

John M. Fahey, Jr., *President and Chief Executive
Officer;* Gilbert M. Grosvenor, *Chairman of the Board;*
Nina D. Hoffman, Executive Vice President, *President
of Book Publishing Group*

Staff for This Book

Nancy Laties Feresten, *Vice President, Editor-in-Chief
of Children's Books*
Virginia Ann Koeth, *Project Editor*
Bea Jackson, *Director of Design and Illustration*
David M. Seager, *Art Director*
Lori Epstein, Greta Arnold, National Geographic Image
Sales, *Illustrations Editors*
Jean Cantu, *Illustrations Specialist*

Carl Mehler, *Director of Maps*
Priyanka Lamichhane, *Assistant Editor*
R. Gary Colbert, *Production Director*
Lewis R. Bassford, *Production Manager*
Vincent P. Ryan, Maryclare Tracy, *Manufacturing
Managers*

For the Brown Reference Group, plc
Tim Cooke, *Managing Editor*
Alan Gooch, *Book Designer*

Photo Credits
Front: © Maria Stenzel/National Geographic Image
Collection Back: © Archeological Museum Lima/
Mireille Vautier/The Art Archive Spine: © Galen
Rowell/ Corbis Background Image: gds/sefa/Corbis

Uncredited pictures are © William Albert Allard/
National Geographic Image Collection

NGIC = National Geographic Image Collection

1, © Archeological Museum Lima/ Mireille Vautier/The
Art Archive; 4, © Werner Forman Archive/Corbis; 6, ©
Galen Rowell/Corbis; 8, © Johan Reinhard; 10, © Ira
Block/NGIC; 11 left, © Stephen Alvarez/NGIC; 11 right,
© Robert S. Oakes & Victor R. Boswell/NGIC; 12–13, ©
Stephen Alvarez/ NGIC; 14–15, © Gordon Wiltsie/
NGIC; 15 left, Museum Fur Volkerkunde, Berlin/
Werner Forman Archive; 15 right, © AKG-Images; 16,
© Keren Su/ Corbis; 17 top, © Kenneth Garrett/NGIC;
17 bottom, © Museum Fur Volkerkunde, Berlin/Werner
Forman Archive; 18–19, © Ira Block/ NGIC; 20 top, ©
Ira Block/ NGIC; 20 bottom, © Ira Block/NGIC; 21, ©
Ira Block/ NGIC; 22 bottom, © British Museum/Werner
Forman Archive; 24 top, Ira Block/NGIC; 24 bottom, ©
David Bernstein/Werner Forman Archive; 25, Alejandro
Balaquer/Stone/ Getty Images; 26, © Museum Fur
Volkerkunde, Berlin/ Werner Forman Archive; 27 top, ©
Museo Pedro de Osma Lima/Mireille Vautier/The Art
Archive; 27 bottom, © Ned Seidler/ NGIC; 31 bottom,
Donald A. Mackay/NGIC; 32, © Ullstein Bild/KPA/
Media colors/AKG-Images; 33, © Nick Saunders/Werner
Forman Archive; 34–35, Pablo Corral Vega/ NGIC; 36
top, © Nick Saunders/Werner Forman Archive; 36
bottom, © Museum Fur Volkerkunder, Berlin/Werner
Forman Archive; 37, © Jeremy Horne/Corbis; 38–39,
Ullstein Bild/AKG Images; 43 top, Gordon Wiltsie/
NGIC; 43 bottom, Gordon Wiltsie/NGIC; 44–45 bottom,
© Maria Stenzel/ NGIC; 46, © Stephen Alvarez/NGIC;
47, © Christopher A. Klein/NGIC; 48, © Christopher A.
Klein/NGIC; 49 top, © Maria Stenzel/ NGIC; 49
bottom, Stephen Alvarez/NGIC; 50 top, © Maria
Stenzel/NGIC; 50 bottom, Maria Stenzel/ NGIC; 51 top,
© Stephen Alvarez/NGIC; 51 bottom, © Maria
Stenzel/NGIC; 52, © Constanza Ceruti; 53, © Maria
Stenzel/ NGIC; 54–55, Gordon Wiltsie/NGIC; 56, ©
Biblioteca Nazionale/Marciana Venice/Dagli Orti/The
Art Archive; 57 top, © Gordon Wiltsie/NGIC; 57
bottom, Pablo Corral Vega/NGIC; 63, © Werner
Forman Archive/ Corbis.

Front cover: Golden statue buried with a child sacrific
on the summit of Llullaillaco. **Page 1 and back cover:**
This gold llama was looted from the Inca by the
Spaniards. **Pages 2–3:** A road winds up a hillside in the
Andes mountains.

NATIONAL GEOGRAPHIC
EOGRAPHIC INVESTIGAG
NVESTIGATES NATIONA
ES NATIONAL GEOGRAPH
L GEOGRAPHIC INVESTIG
C INVESTIGATES NATIO
ATES NATIONAL GEOGRA
NAL GEOGRAPHIC INVES
PHIC INVESTIGATES NAT
GATES NATIONAL GEOG
ONAL GEOGRAPHIC INVE
RAPHIC INVESTIGATES N
STIGATES NATIONAL GEO
ATIONAL GEOGRAPHIC I
OGRAPHIC INVESTIGATE
NVESTIGATES NATIONAL
S NATIONAL GEOGRAPHI